How to Develop, Build and Increase Your Momentum

By Landon T. Smith

Copyright 2017 by Landon T. Smith

Published by Make Profits Easy LLC

Profitsdaily123@aol.com

facebook.com/MakeProfitsEasy

Table of Contents

Introduction 4
Chapter 1: Newton's First Law 6
Chapter 2: The Sum of All Habits 16
Chapter 3: Getting In Motion 28
Chapter 4: The Disciplined Mind 44
Chapter 5: Roadblocks to Momentum 62
Conclusion 76

Introduction

What defines a successful individual? There can be a lot of answers to that question, it could be determination, it could be strength of character, force of will or even some kind of innate trait that allows for a person to achieve incredible success. There are half a dozen factors that can determine someone's success in life, but we must ask ourselves, what is the most important factor that can lead to great success in someone's life? That factor is momentum! Indeed, if you look across the board, you can see how momentum can have a monumental impact in a person's life.

What is momentum? For the purpose of this book, we define momentum as the increase of results gained by continuing to press forward and refusing to stop. For example, let's consider a football game. When a team suddenly starts doing well, they tend to gain momentum, each successful play increases that momentum and it presses them forward, to eventually win the game. Momentum is as psychological as it is physical. We're going to be covering all of the different ways that momentum can affect you in your life, for the better. We're going to look at the things that increase momentum, speed you up, lead to incredible success in your life and above all, will keep you moving forward. We're also going to be taking a look at the various different techniques that you can use to maintain momentum and then we're also going to be speaking about the momentum killers that can destroy your chances of success if you aren't careful. If you've always wanted to reach massive success in your life, but could never seem to get there, then maybe all you need is a little bit of momentum!

Chapter 1: Newton's First Law

Famed physicist, Isaac Newton, wrote a series of laws that were designed to govern basic physical truths. One such law was Newton's First Law: An object at rest tends to stay at rest, while an object in motion tends to stay in motion, until acted upon by some external force. And there lies our formula for success! It might seem a little strange at first, to use a physics law to understand the law of success, but let's break it down.

An Object at Rest:

Let's think about energy for a moment. Momentum is all about the use and movement of energy. Think about how hard it is to get up in the morning, when you first wake up. Think of how tough it can be to motivate yourself to go to the gym, or how hard it is to get going on some big research project. When we are in a restful state, we tend to stay that way until there is some kind of pressure to get into motion. The longer we are at rest, the harder it is for us to get motivated. This is due to the fact that we tend to have different mental modes and our brains usually prefer to stay in one mode at a time. This is why when a person is in relaxation mode, they tend to just want to rest and enjoy themselves.

The problem is when our desire to stay at rest directly impacts our ability to get stuff done. For example, suppose that you desperately need to clean your apartment, yet you are lying on the couch watching Netflix. You have every intention to clean your apartment, you have a great desire, yet as you watch each episode of Friends, you feel no great urge to get up and clean. So, you procrastinate and stay in your state of relaxation, despite the fact that this state is going to actively harm you in the long run. There are unseen forces of work when we procrastinate, those unseen forces tend to exert pressure on us to keep us staying in our current state. It takes a significant expenditure of energy in order to get moving. So, what are those unseen forces that keep us at rest? They are:

- Emotional Baggage
- Fatigue
- Boredom
- Lack of Inspiration
- Obligation
- Lack of Discipline
- Apathy
- Fear

As you can see from that list, there are quite a few things that could potentially keep us in the same spot. It's important to note that most people don't procrastinate just simply because they are lazy. The word Lazy is a shame-based word designed to cast judgment on other people. It's not a healthy or useful word, because it oversimplifies the problem of what keeps us from getting in motion. If a student doesn't work on his school work because he is "lazy," then we are free to judge him as a bad student. Yet, if we were to break down what the real reasons for his procrastination, we might find that he struggles immensely with it due to the difficulty, or he is afraid of failure, or that he isn't happy with the subject matter. By calling someone lazy, we are ignoring all of the potential things that are going on inside of a person and we are oversimplifying the problem.

So, what happens when we call ourselves lazy? We are just trying to over simplify our own problems and will never really become successful. Why is that? Well, if the only reason you are refusing to do your big project is because you are lazy, then the only solution is for you to become "not lazy" and how would you even start doing that? By learning to identify the hidden forces that keep us procrastinating, it allows us to overcome them without having to resort to simply calling ourselves lazy. Once we have identified what is holding us back and we've sufficiently dealt with it, we then have the ability to maintain momentum.

An object in motion tends to stay at motion:

Have you ever felt like you didn't want to exercise, but when you started, you found that it was incredibly easy to keep going? Have you ever dreaded doing a schoolwork assignment, but found out that once you began, it was easier to keep going? This is essentially the essence of momentum. Once we begin working toward something, it tends to get easier to stay in motion. Why is that? Because our minds shift gears once again. Artists, athletes and musicians tend to experience this rather often, it's known as the Flow, a state of mind where they are intensely focused and in the zone. A person doesn't reach that state of momentum automatically, they must work to get there, but when it happens, it tends to be an incredible experience. Have you ever been lost in a book or a movie? Have you ever been so focused in a conversation that time literally blinked by? Momentum tends to accelerate our perception of time due to the fact that we feel like we are completely absorbed by what we are doing.

How does momentum influence our success? Well think about it! If you are a student, trying desperately to get your thesis paper done, you're going to need momentum in order to achieve victory, you're going to need to A. Get in motion and B. Stay in motion, in order to get your paper done. Momentum is the polar opposite of procrastination. When you procrastinate, you are shooting yourself in the foot, but when you begin to work, you begin to generate momentum. It is that momentum that will define how much you can get done and how often you can get it done. A man who's trying to build up a small business needs momentum to increase every single day so that he can get all of his tasks and jobs done. A woman who's trying to get fit will need momentum in her workouts so that she can increase in fitness and intensity with each passing day.

Momentum isn't a singular event, rather it is something that occurs over time. Consider a snowball. When a snowball begins to roll down a hill, it begins to increase in momentum. As it rolls faster, it begins to collect more snow and increase in mass, increasing its size as well as its momentum. Eventually that little snowball will become a rather large one as it barrels down the hill. While many times we hear the words "snowball effect" as a bad thing, when it comes to building momentum, we view the snowball effect as a very good thing. Imagine that little snowball is whatever you want to accomplish on day one. If you keep at it and continue working, eventually your little idea will grow into something huge and will bring you the success that you desire.

If momentum is so powerful and can bring us success, why is it so hard to accumulate?

Well, it's because of the sentence in Newton's First Law.

...unless acted upon by an outside force

There are things in this world that serve only to kill our momentum. They are wide and varied, no case is the same. Some people can be disrupted by their lack of motivation, others can be disrupted by real life getting in the way of their goals. Momentum is valuable to reach success in life, but when we get hit by something that blocks our way, it tends to kill our momentum. Then we revert back to that natural state of sitting around or procrastinating. This is more or less how things work for regular people. They have bursts of momentum, followed by an interruption, which then leads to a long period of inactivity or procrastination. Then, they are able to overcome those forces for a brief moment, leading them to make strides in their career or fitness life, until they are hit by another momentum killer. This vicious cycle plays itself over and over again in perpetuity.

Many industries make a killing off of this lifestyle. The internet Guru industry tries to convince people that the reason why they failed is because they don't have the right "system" and that for a cheap purchase of 200 dollars, they can have the perfect business system that will make them successful. The health industry claims that you don't have the right diet program, or right exercise regime, or that you need some kind of magical pill in order to get fit. The reality is that these industries are just taking advantage of that natural start-stop cycle and won't really do much other than provide a person with fuel for a little bit before they burn out.

The key to gaining momentum isn't buying some expensive product, or taking pills, or using some kind of scientific mumbo jumbo to lifehack your way to victory, the key to gaining momentum is learning why we exist in stop-start cycles and learn how to break the pattern in order to achieve maximum greatness. Indeed, you will find that the truth is that patterns and habits are the key to building momentum in your life.

Chapter 2: The Sum of All Habits

Aristotle once said "We are what we repeatedly do, excellence then is not an act, but a habit." Many of us are looking for some kind of clever trick or magic bullet that will turn us into momentum machines. We tend to look for some kind of change in circumstances, or some sort of special technique that will allow us to circumvent our natural desires and turn us into successful people overnight. Yet, that kind of attitude entirely ignores why we as people tend to be stuck in the start-stop cycle. The reason we get stuck in that pattern is because it is the sum of our habits.

A habit, more or less, is something that you do on a regular basis. It is an automatic way of acting. For example, some people like to chew on their nails. In fact, someone who chews on their nails as a habit might not even notice that they are doing so, mainly because habits tend to be relatively automatic. Our brains are extremely good at learning from patterns and developing habits from those patterns. The more you do something, the more the brain comes to believe that that action is necessary. So, the brain creates stronger neural pathways that make the actions more automatic. The more you consciously repeat a habit, the more your brain stores that information away. Eventually, even when you aren't fully focusing, you will begin to automatically act according to your habits.

We tend to see this the most in bad habits. Someone who oversleeps every single day of their life tends to be seen as someone who has bad habits, while someone who wakes up at 5am each morning is usually seen as someone who has good habits. We don't want to use the word good or bad habits here, because really, obligation doesn't particularly help when it comes to developing new goals or habits. If we let ourselves be driven by our desire to comply with external standards, our hearts tend not to be in it. So rather than say good or bad, let's say desired. You probably have undesired habits and desired habits. We all do. Some people desire to be morning people and have habits based around going to sleep early. Some people desire to hang out and play video games instead of doing homework, so their habits are formed around reaching for their game controller.

When we begin to look at habits as rooted in our desire, we start to see where the rubber hits the road. How many of us desire to be out of shape slobs who can't take care of ourselves? I would wager to say that there probably aren't any people who desire to be that way. Yet their habits might end up keeping them in that lifestyle. This is where we must acknowledge what we desire and then go about setting new habits. Yet, there is usually a problem. Due to our culture and the way we negatively perceive the world, we tend to think in negatives when it comes to forming habits. For example, if someone wants to wake up earlier, they might set a goal as "I don't want to oversleep anymore."

This kind of goal for a new habit isn't very good due to the fact that the brain doesn't have the ability to not think of something. I'll prove it: don't think of a purple elephant. No matter what you did, there was no way for you to stop yourself from thinking about that elephant. So, when a person sets a goal based out of a negative, their brain doesn't do a particularly good job of avoiding thinking about that negative. This essentially sabotages you from the very beginning.

There is no such thing as habit removal. The brain is an incredibly complex machine and is designed to perfectly process information, keeping everything where it needs to be so that when you live your daily life, you will be able to use the patterns and models in order to be able to survive. The brain does not willingly remove any information or pattern from its mind. However, that doesn't mean that we can't change. It means that we must change the way we think about how habits work. If we cannot remove a habit, then it means that we must be able to *replace* the habit. The brain is somewhat adaptable to new information replacing old information, but it will require repetition in order to get things really hammered in. The younger a person is, the easier it is for them to learn because there is no information in their heads, but the older a person gets, the harder it is for them to overcome their biases and conclusions. This is just because the brain wants to make sure that nothing gets forgotten, as keeping all of your memories, ideas and information intact will keep you alive.

Replacement of a habit focuses on learning something new and committing to focusing on it until you have it down. For example, if you want to wake up early, you must have the habit of waking up every morning at 5am, regardless of how you feel. This habit for the first few weeks will be extremely hard due to the fact that the brain is far more interested in maintaining its current habits. This is what makes change so tough for us. Our brains aren't particularly elastic when we are older and the formation of new habits tend to take longer. The average amount of time to form a habit is 66 days. That's not short at all, it's more than two months and it takes that much time before you begin to do something automatically.

So how do habits interact with our momentum? Well, let's think about those forces once again. Many of the forces that prevent us from achieving our goals tend to be external, right? If you want to get fit, you will work out every day, but what if you sprain your ankle, or if you can't make it to the gym due to a meeting that's late? We tend to view the things that disrupt our patterns as being the problem, but the reality is that many times we just haven't established a habit that supports us yet. See, the start-stop cycle that most of us fall victim to exists because we haven't developed supporting habits quite yet. So, we get excited to start our new gym routine, but end up skipping a day.

Then we skip two more, then we stop going entirely. Our momentum is dead. But a person who has a habit of going to the gym is still capable of enduring hiccups and occasionally missing out without losing their momentum.

This means that if we are going to build great momentum in our lives, then we must be able to develop habits that support our own momentum. No one wakes up in the morning and says "I think I'll develop a habit of procrastinating before work and watching TV." What happens is that these habits occur over time, the more a person acts a certain way, the more reinforced it becomes. The habit forms over time and before it's too late, we become defined by that habit. The amount of exertion required to change that habit is immense and can be exhausting, but most of all, it must be intentional. Most of our habits are formed unconsciously, so we must make the decision to form them consciously. Once we realize that we are in control of our own habits, once we take responsibility for our habits, we can begin to change them for the better. Let's take a look at a series of steps that you can take in the formation of a new habit.

Habit Forming Step 1: Identify Desired Outcome

The first step to developing any kind of new habit is to be able to identify your desired outcome. For example, if you want to wake up earlier, you should write out that you want to wake up at a certain time. Being specific is extremely important when it comes to developing a habit because specifics give you no wiggle room. Saying "I'll wake up earlier," is a lot more laid back than saying "I'll wake up at 5," the more wiggle room you give a habit, the easier it is to not actually do it. By being specific with your desired habit, you are ensuring that you are setting yourself up for success!

Habit Forming Step 2: Commitment

A habit is not something to be taken lightly. The creation of a new habit is akin to taking care of a baby animal or an actual baby, you must be willingly to watch over it, care for it and nurse it to life. If you refuse to commit to your habit, it will quickly die. The habit must be cared for intensely and this requires you to be fully committed to seeing your habit come to fruition.

This can be an exhaustive effort, by the way. See, a habit is automatic after a while, so it takes very little willpower to maintain. Yet at the very beginning of a habit-forming system, you're going to have to use a lot of willpower to establish that habit. Commitment must be total, or else you might find yourself growing tempted to give up, to neglect it or worse, just put it off until tomorrow. You must find the willpower within to stick with your habits and that requires a commitment.

Habit Forming Step 3: Consistency

Spring boarding off of commitment, you're going to need to spend a good enough amount of time actually maintaining your new habit. This means that you're going to need to use reminders, a conscious effort to do your habit on a daily basis and stay accountable. One great way to gain consistency is to make efforts to let another person know that you are going to be doing something new and that you would like them to keep you accountable. When you make arrangements to do some changes in your own head, it is very easy to slack off. When you make arrangements to make some changes and you tell a friend about it, it's a bit harder.

Habit Forming Step 4: Track and Adjust

Sometimes a goal that you might have is unrealistic. Sometimes you might find that you aren't particularly happy with the results. Just because you set out on a goal to change your habit doesn't mean you have to stick with it if it's detrimental or doesn't work out for you. It's important to track the results of your new habit and if you see that it's causing you trouble or if it isn't garnering the good results that you want, you might need to adjust. It's better to make changes to a habit while you're still forming it than it is to have to deal with later on.

So, in summation, habits are essentially the building blocks of momentum. If you want to be able to attain fantastic momentum, you must be able to build good habits. Of course, momentum looks different across the board. Someone who's focusing on improving their health will have wildly different habits from someone who's trying to write a book. So, don't think that there is some perfect selection of habits that you can figure out that will allow you to be successful across the board. You're going to have to focus on building one habit at a time, as a support network to your main goals.

Chapter 3: Getting In Motion

After you have spent enough time thinking about your habits, we must now consider the initial act of getting into motion. Momentum is easy enough to maintain once you have it, but the biggest trouble in most people's lives is being able to get moving. So how do we get into motion? Well, the first step is to understand the *why* of getting into motion.

Many of us desire to do something important with our lives. We want to get involved with a charity, or start a business, write a book or get in shape. It's very easy to get caught up in a lot of reasons for why we should do something important looking, but it's also easy to be motivated by the wrong reasons. If you don't have a strong reason to get into motion, it can be extremely hard to be motivated to get going. There are lots of reasons to do things, but sometimes you need to find the reason that works best for you.

Imagine the difference between the student who wants to go to school to become a lawyer versus the student who is going to college because his parents are forcing him to. They might both be going to the same school, attending the same classes, but their behavior is going to be very different. It's because they have a much different reason for being there. The boy who always wanted to be a lawyer is driven by an intense desire to fulfill his purpose, so it makes it easier for him to sit down and do his school work, to show up to class, to study for the exams. The boy who's being sent there by his parents under duress won't have any of those reasons to motivate him. The ability to gain and maintain momentum must come from an extremely strong reason. It must come from a very powerful why.

So, who is responsible for developing a strong reason? Why, it's you of course! You are responsible for developing and understanding the reasons for your actions. You must be able to look at your intentions and ideas, asking yourself if you seriously want it. Not only must you ask if you want it, you must ask why you want it. Are you wanting to write a book because you want to be rich and famous? Do you want a small business because you are sick and tired of being someone else's lackey? There are no wrong answers when it comes to motivation, because as you seek to gain momentum, you are going to need motivation more than anything else in the world.

Motivation is one of the most powerful tools in your life. When it comes to gaining momentum, you must look at motivation as the gunpowder that will fire you forward in your life. The more motivated you are, the more likely you will be to act. The less motivated you are, the harder it will be to act. So, we must come to understand that motivation is the single most important thing you can have at your disposal when it comes to starting to move forward.

How does motivation work for the majority of us? Well, motivation usually comes sporadically or at the very least, on occasion. Many of us suffer from a chronic lack of motivation. There are so many things in this world that work to strip us of our motivation in life. We have to deal with putting our big plans on pause while real life gets in the way. Other people might tell us that we can't, or worse, we might have developed the unhealthy habit of telling ourselves that we can't do what we want to do. So, every now and then we might experience a burst of motivation, but for the most part we live our lives woefully undernourished in this area. The reason that we have so little nourishment when it comes to motivation is primarily because we tend not to realize our responsibility in our own motivation.

Motivation is not some kind of rare event that happens without any kind of warning. Motivation is not a lightning strike, nor is it some kind of phenomenon that happens on its own. We must look at motivation as if it were a plant. When you have your initial idea, whatever it may be, there tends to be a major burst of energy and excitement. That energy becomes like fuel to your mind and soon you are busy working as hard as you can on whatever that project is. Perhaps it's a book, maybe it's an exciting new relationship or it might even be a website. The energy and motivation provided by the excitement of the newness makes it very easy to leap out of bed and get right to work, but at some point, that energy will fade away. As the energy fades, it will significantly affect your ability to get things done. Your momentum slows down and soon a project that you were so sure was going to be the next most important thing in your life gets shelved. You grow bored. Some of us might even think that it was a bad idea since all of that energy is gone and so we move onto something new. Nothing can ever get done that way, can it?

When we have those great ideas, those plans, it's like we plant a beautiful little seed in the ground. That seed is motivation and if we treat it right, it will grow bigger and bigger, providing us with all of the energy that we need to complete our task. But what if we ignore our motivation and just work? Well, it doesn't particularly grow and so when we run out of energy, we're out. The difference between success and failure when it comes to momentum is highly dependent on how you view your motivation.

Many us of view motivation as an external event. We think that it arrives, stays for a bit and then goes on its merry way. The reality is that our motivation levels must come from within. You are, more or less, entirely responsible for your motivation level at all times. This means that it is up to you to find the things that inspire you, to stoke the flames until you are ready to keep moving, no matter what. If you want to have the most amount of momentum in your life, you're going to have to stay motivated. Motivation is the fuel for your engine, but most of us don't look at it like that. We don't realize that we have to constantly be refueling or else we'll end up running out of steam. And so, we run with what little fuel we have, then when we run out, we throw away our dreams or plans *instead* of seeking more fuel. This is mindboggling, but it is also the primary reason why most people fail when they set out to achieve some kind of task. It's not because they are incompetent, or lazy, or dumb, it's because they don't have the ability to motivate themselves properly. They were never taught that they are responsible for their own motivations and in the process, they lose a valuable tool.

If you learn how to keep yourself motivated, you will have one of the most valuable possible abilities in all of the world. You will have the ability to build and maintain your momentum with ease. Motivation is that major factor that inspires us to achieve great things in our lives. So how do we build up our own motivation? Where do we start? Is it some kind of magical process? Not at all. The process of becoming motivated is all about learning where to look. It's about finding the things that inspire you and continuously looking for those things to keep you moving. Let's look at a good process of finding motivation in your life.

Motivation Tip 1: Figure out what you like

It might seem a little obvious at first, but the most important step you can take when you're learning how to keep yourself motivated is to find the things that you respond to the most. There are many different types of motivational content that exists, but not everyone is motivated by the same things. There are people in this world who can be motivated by strong emotional stories that get their heartstrings tugged and there are people in this world who can be motivated by reading war stories. The most important thing to remember is that motivation is not a universal rule. Everyone is moved by something different.

You've got to be able to determine what moves you. Have you ever spent any time really asking what are the things that inspire you? Maybe it's a good Disney movie. Perhaps it's some kind of podcast, or daily blog. You've got to find the sources of inspiration that keep you going in the hard times. Think about what is inspiring you to do what you are doing. Look at the seeds of motivation that are planted deep inside of your heart. Are you wanting to work really hard because you want to retire early and travel? Read financial advice and travel blogs daily. Do you want to become a filmmaker? Watch really good movies, movies that are so moving that they convince you to get up and start working.

Motivation Tip 2: Motivation brings movement

It's important not to confuse motivation with feeling good. There are many things in this world that make us feel good but don't necessarily inspire us to get going. A good source of motivation is something that makes you feel like getting something done, even if you didn't feel like it earlier. So, make sure that you aren't oversaturating yourself with nice, feel-good messages that don't get you moving. You need to find sources that will get you excited enough to get off the couch and get going. It's the difference between a movie that makes you feel happy and a podcast that has you furiously writing afterwards. Focus on finding the things that elicit movement, not the things that make you cheered up.

Motivation Tip 3: Focus on Similar Areas

One great way to keep yourself energized and moving forward in your life is to look for areas of inspiration that are similar to your story. If you're someone who's trying to get involved in the fashion world, perhaps it would be a good idea to find stories of people who made it, or better yet find other people who are currently fighting to get somewhere in fashion. The idea is that part of motivation is about hearing the struggles that other people are going through as they work to reach success. You don't always need to hear a story about how someone managed to become a millionaire by 25 without any kind of major hiccups or failures. Many times, we can respond more to a story where we hear of the difficulties and odds that sincerely got in a person's way or about the time a famous person had even given up on his current job.

Negative stories can help as well. Don't think that motivation is all about hearing good things happen. Sometimes you need a reality check, sometimes in order to keep your momentum you need to read tales of failure. Sometimes there might be stories of failure that don't have a rebound, sometimes you'll find a story about someone who never was able to achieve their dreams. These things can be destructive if you aren't careful, but don't think that just because there are some sources of information that seem a bit dismal doesn't meant that you can't learn from them. The more you learn, the more you are able to avoid past mistakes.

Motivation Tip 4: Never Stop Learning

One important way to keep yourself motivated is to dedicate some time at the beginning of your day and focus on learning as much as you can about your given field. Many extremely successful people have dedicated themselves to this. Mark Cuban, famous entrepreneur and investor on the television show Shark Tank often speaks about the value of reading books every day. He says that those who don't read are missing out on the most important and valuable information that you could possibly have in your life. By having a daily pursuit of learning, you will naturally keep your motivation levels up at all times. The more you focus on learning, the easier it will be to navigate through various pitfalls of whatever you are trying to achieve.

This is where a healthy habit can come into play. By learning to develop a daily habit and regimen of consuming a few sources of information, be it a book, blog or news article, you can add tons of productivity and momentum to your day. As the old adage goes, measure twice, cut once. The best thing you can do for yourself each day is to spend some time growing yourself in knowledge and wisdom. Then you can move forward with the many things that you need to do each day.

Motivation Tip 5: Reward Yourself

In any serious endeavor, there are things that are extremely fun and there are things that are very boring. Professional football players enjoy the football games that they play, but there's no doubt that they get a little bored during the hundreds of hours of training leading up to every game. There are things in any profession that are rewards unto themselves and there are things that are more or less like chores. You will find that we tend to be very motivated for the rewarding moments and we tend to lose our motivation when we have to do the boring things. There aren't really easy ways to make boring tasks fun, so make sure that you create some kind of system where you actively reward yourself for your willingness to do the boring thing. If you have to spend the next four days editing, promise yourself some kind of small indulgence, or trip. Focus on using basic motivational techniques to convince yourself to stay motivated and excited as you do things that aren't particularly enjoyable. Not everything has to be fun, but it's usually the boring tasks that tend to lead to the greatest successes in life.

Motivation Tip 6: Create Attainable Small Goals

Small, attainable goals will essentially allow for you to maintain your motivation on a daily basis by giving you small victories. Each time we achieve a goal, our brain sends signals that make us feel good. The brain has a great love of achievement and the satisfaction that comes from achieving just about any goal is valuable when it comes to keeping your motivation up. So, make sure that whatever you are working towards, you keep your momentum going by having a list of goals that you are working to attain. Each time you see a goal checked off, it will give you more inspiration and motivation with your life.

Motivation Tip 7: Create Visuals

One of the easiest ways to keep your motivation tank full is to create some kind of system to where you can see your goals, ideas and dreams first thing in the morning. This might involve putting some kind of checklist on your mirror or an inspirational poster in your bedroom. Perhaps it involves you making a collage of all of your goals in a visual manner. We are visual creatures and so whenever we see something that creates a feeling of motivation and inspiration, it can increase our natural desire to get involved in those tasks.

As you see, the key to not only getting started but also staying in motivation lies within our motivations. The more motivated we are, the easier it is to stay the course. On the flipside, of course, the less motivated we are, the better chance we have of abandoning our plans. Yet, while motivation is one of the most important pieces to the puzzle, it is not the only piece. Yes, there are other areas that we must be willing to look at if we want to keep our momentum going at all times. One such area is the area of discipline.

Chapter 4: The Disciplined Mind

So now that we've seen that one of the most important elements of starting your momentum is motivation, you're probably wondering if that is all it takes. Not quite. The act of continuing to move forward, regardless of external circumstances requires a combination of energy and discipline. Motivation will provide you with the energy, but discipline will provide you with the strength to achieve the things that are relatively hard to achieve.

If you ask any great man how he became great, he will tell you that it was through a combination of luck, cleverness and discipline. No matter how much it might look like it from the outside, no one ever achieves anything worthwhile without discipline. Discipline is essentially the glue that holds everything together for you. If you want to achieve greatness without discipline, then you will only achieve momentary success. You can't build momentum in a short amount of time, in fact, you will find that it takes quite some time to build up real momentum. In order to achieve great things over time, you have to have discipline.

Consider how a small business works. When the owner starts up his company, he must have immense discipline in order to get his business growing. Each time he achieves his goals, his momentum increases a little bit. After several years of hard work, his discipline allows him to continue working through the tougher times. Motivation plays a major role in the *why* of his actions, but discipline plays a bigger role in *how* he achieves his goals.

Discipline is essentially the ability to train yourself to do the necessary tasks in your life. The greatest example of discipline can often be found in martial arts. For a martial artist to achieve incredible feats of physical strength and control, they must have a very disciplined mind. It's not enough for them to be strong, they must have total control over their own bodies and the only way they can get that control is through discipline. Likewise, if we want to have the momentum to get things done, we must have the discipline to consistently work. We must be able to train ourselves to do the tasks that we need to do and we must train ourselves to be consistent. These things aren't particularly easy, which is why discipline is the key to success.

As stated before, there really is no magic bullet when it comes to learning how to gain momentum. There are no external circumstances that will increase your momentum or your day to day victories. To rely on external circumstances is essentially to give up your own role in achievement. There are always going to be things in your life that will cause you trouble. You might have problems securing financing for your company, you might hit writer's block, you may even end up having to deal with some kind of personal tragedy of some sort. There are literally thousands of ways that external circumstances can prevent you from achieving your dreams, but once again, we must state that the externals will always be there to threaten you in some way. A strong internal strength is necessary to overcome these external things that will prevent you from keeping your momentum. One of those internal things is the internal practice of discipline.

Okay, so discipline is important. How do we develop discipline and what does discipline look like in everyday life? Well, the first step to developing discipline is to make a commitment to learning to overcome our natural desire for comfort. In our modern society, we find that we have a great desire for comfort due to the fact that our culture stresses being comfortable beyond all other things. Comfort is king, as people often believe and so they spend their lives seeking out comfort in just about any way possible. This leads a person to search for nicer and nicer things, but it also causes them to move away from the things that cause us to be uncomfortable. This is problematic, though, because discomfort is often a great way to grow in strength and character. Consider the stairs versus the elevator. Many people prefer to take the elevator due to the fact that it is far more comfortable. The elevator is nice, air conditioned and moves us to our destination with no strain on our muscles or cardiovascular system. Consequently, the stairs will often cause us to breathe heavily as we ascend up them, our hearts will pound and if the stairs are far enough, they very well could cause us to break a sweat. One is much more comfortable than the other, but the question is: which one is better for you? In reality, taking the stairs will increase your physical ability, despite the fact that it is very uncomfortable for the time being. Such a small decision can actually have a massive impact on you if you lived your life in such a way as to be willing to consider uncomfortable situations as long as they provide benefits.

Make no mistake, in the world of momentum, there will be plenty of times where you will be tempted with comfort. Most famous people did not achieve great things by getting a healthy sleep schedule, or by spending all of their money eating out at restaurants. They usually got where they did by making the uncomfortable sacrifices that caused temporary pain but would lead to long-lasting success. This is what makes discipline the separating factor between success and failure. Those who are only looking for comfort will most likely give up the moment they are required to do something that is wildly uncomfortable. It's not particularly easy to take the stairs, but it is way more effective in the long run.

So, comfort and discipline are often at odds. This isn't to say that there is something wrong with comfort, because that would be ludicrous. There is something wrong with seeking out comfort to your own detriment. If you are faced with the choice between taking the comfortable route or taking the uncomfortable route that will lead you to something greater down the road, you must be willing to walk down that uncomfortable road and that takes discipline.

Discipline is essentially the ability to train yourself to endure discomfort as you seek after some kind of higher purpose. The goal isn't to be uncomfortable for discomfort's sake, the goal is to get to something great, but doing so would require you to be in a state of discomfort for quite some time. So, that is why you need discipline if you want to keep your momentum going. So how can we develop more discipline in our lives? Well, let's take a look:

Discipline Development Step 1: Ignore the temptations.

Feelings can be clever little liars designed to trick you into submitting to your habits. Whenever we begin to move out of our habits, our feelings begin to try and convince us that we should go back to what we know. When you are getting out of bed first thing in the morning, your feelings try to convince you that you absolutely need to go back to sleep or else you'll be too tired. When you're on a diet and you walk past a pretzel stand in the mall, your stomach will try to convince you that you feel like having a delicious carby pretzel. The reality is that our feelings are often temporary things and don't tell us the full story. While it's important to acknowledge the reality that you feel a certain way, whenever a temptation arrives, don't trust how you feel. Your feelings will often try to convince you to do the comfortable thing. This is a byproduct of living in a comfort driven society. The more focused we are on our comfort, the easier it is to give into the temptation to indulge ourselves.

There are many different sources of temptation that exist, things that can pull us away from the things that are important to us. You must be able to identify your weaknesses and as you develop your discipline, make a point of working to avoid those temptations. If you are trying to cut back on alcohol while you spend your time working on a major project, avoid hanging out in bars. If you're needing to work late in the night, find a place where you can work that isn't near your bed. Temptations will constantly barrage you and your feelings will try to convince you that you need to obey your impulses, but the reality is that each time we resist these impulses, we develop a stronger sense of discipline. We develop the habit of self-control.

Discipline Development Step 2: Physically Challenge Yourself

There are many lessons that can be learned from a physical challenge. When a person pushes themselves physically, they often learn many different lessons about themselves. They learn their breaking point, they learn how to endure, they learn how to keep going in spite of how they feel. In other words, when a person physically trains themselves, they increase their natural level of mental discipline. Many people make the mistake of thinking that physical training is a purely physical thing and thus they write it off as somewhat useless. Indeed, if the entire purpose of running, weightlifting or kickboxing was to improve yourself physically, then it would be understandable that many people would prefer not to deal with the headache. Yet, the reality is that physical exercise is one of the most powerful ways to stay strong and motivated due to the fact that there are a ton of benefits to be had from physical exercise.

The biggest benefit is that exercise acts as a mood booster to your body, increasing powerful endorphins that reduce stress, increase relaxation and even improve your thinking power. Many people who regularly exercise experience a significant increase in discipline due to the fact that exercise is often very uncomfortable at times. This is a great way to learn how to push through things that you don't necessarily enjoy. The physical challenge of working out will more or less increase your focus and resolve, which in the long term will help contribute to the higher level of discipline in your life.

They key to increasing discipline through physical exercise is learning how to push yourself to the point where you would normally quit. It's not necessarily about doing exercises that you hate, rather it's about taking whatever your preferred type of workout is and focusing on pushing past your physical limits. We often *feel* like we cannot keep going, but the reality is that tends to really just be in our minds. Our body will let us know when we cannot keep pushing, mainly because it will stop working, but anything before that is really just our minds giving up. By regularly trying to push past your own limits, you will find your natural willpower increasing. So, try increasing the intensity of whatever your preferred workout is. If you like to jog, set a distance or time goal that you would struggle to achieve. If you are a weightlifter, pick some weight goals that will really strain you (safely of course,) regardless of what you do, if you try to increase intensity, you will benefit significantly.

Discipline Development Step 3: No Excuses

Once again, the word consistency comes up. I cannot emphasize enough how important it is to focus on being consistent with all of your actions. Part of discipline is having the strength to do something day in and day out, never deviating from the schedule. If you are trying to write a book, it means that you must be willing to work every single day until the book is completed. If you're trying to lose weight, then it means you must have the willingness and consistency to keep your diet at all times. In order to develop a discipline that keeps you consistent, you must be willing to make the sacrifices of comfort and keep to your schedule. This means that you must be willing not to believe any of the excuses that you will naturally produce when you want to do something that goes against your long-term goals. Sometimes we can be our own worst enemy when it comes to achievement, after all, we are the ones who indulge in desserts when we should be eating healthy, we are the ones who sleep in when it's time to get up and we're the ones who stay up late when we have something important to do early in the morning.

There is, within everyone, two selves: the undisciplined self and the disciplined self. Many times, these two selves within us begin to argue with one another. It can be akin to a toddler arguing with its parents over something. We must learn to ignore all of the excuses that our undisciplined self will try to argue with us. "You deserve this treat!" it might say, or "we've worked really hard this week, why don't we just take it easy instead?" These inner dialogues might happen at a moment's notice and will provide with us an extreme temptation. Try to commit yourself to a singular rule of never giving into an excuse that suddenly comes up. There is nothing wrong with planning days of rest ahead of time, the problem is when spontaneity is involved. The spontaneous self often sabotages us, so we must be wary of anything that just suddenly comes into our minds.

The tough thing about discipline is that no one else will hold us accountable for our own internal actions. Yes, sometimes we'll have to face the consequences of living an undisciplined life, but for the most part, the war will be entirely internal. This means that you must be willing to ignore that voice that will often try to discourage you and instead work to create a much stronger inner voice, one that is reasonable and disciplined. When you hear the case for why you should eat that ice cream rise up inside your head, you must be willing to argue fervently for why you shouldn't consume that dessert. This leads to discipline and keeps you consistent across the board.

Discipline Development Step 4: Bring a Friend

Accountability can be one of the most powerful forces on earth, if you do it right. There are many different ways to be held accountable as you seek to develop discipline, but perhaps one of the best ways is to find a friend who is willing to help you succeed by assisting you in reaching your goals. You will find that the more you work alongside someone else who has the same goals or aspirations, the easier it is to get in sync and stay disciplined. This means that it would be of your greatest benefit to find someone who would be interested in whatever it is your doing. If you're trying to lose weight, find a partner who can ask you how your diet's going. If you want to get in shape, find a friend who has similar goals, or better yet, find a friend who's already fit and can teach you stuff. There is a ton of value in finding relationships that will keep you honest and strong throughout your work.

The more support that you have in your life, the easier it will be for you to keep your momentum.

There can, of course, be a danger in inviting other people into helping you develop more discipline. One of the biggest dangers can be inviting potentially damaging or destructive people. You want folks who can push you forward and encourage you, you don't want to have people who will mock you, tease you or worse, try to shame you into doing better. The fact is, people respond much better to positive reinforcement than they do to negative reinforcement, and those who seek to belittle you when you fail won't achieve the desired effect of motivating you, if anything, it will just cause you to do even worse.

Discipline Development Step 5: Just Do It.

The reality of discipline is the fact that it is ultimately similar to a muscle. The only real way to make a muscle stronger is to work out. Discipline is the exact same way, the only way to become more disciplined is to work at your discipline. There will be days that you fail and there will be days that you succeed. The goal is to eventually have far more subsequent days of success than to days of failure. Many times, people can get caught up in the idea that there is some kind of magical technique that can make a person way more disciplined, but that's not particularly true. There is no method of increasing discipline past practicing it on a daily basis. You can read plenty of literature on discipline, you can study it and learn all sorts of interesting techniques, but if you don't make an active practice towards increasing your discipline, you will find that all that learning doesn't really amount to much. No matter how much you read on the subject, you will never become more disciplined without practice. Just do it and keep doing it until you are able to achieve all of the goals that you want to achieve.

Well, that's pretty much it when it comes to increasing your discipline in life. If motivation is the fuel for your momentum, then discipline is the vehicle that will allow you to get to your actual destination. Yet, before we close out, there is still one area that absolutely must be talked about: the things that threaten to kill your momentum in life.

Chapter 5: Roadblocks to Momentum

Perhaps at this point you have seen the tremendous value in learning how to keep your inspiration and motivation high. You've learned the value of building good habits and you know that you need discipline in order to reach a level of pivotal success in just about any field you put your hands towards. With those elements, you will be able to create a powerful internal fortitude that will allow you to overcome many of the common obstacles in your life that stops a person from reaching their full potential. These three traits, when combined, can make you an absolute machine when it comes to serious achievement. Yet, while we put a great amount of emphasis on internal strength, we must still be willing to look at the internal threats that can stop you from achieving your own goal of having a daily momentum that will ultimately lead you to victory.

What are those internal threats? Well, there are a few and believe it or not, these threats come entirely from the inside. There is a common trend in today's culture to try and blame failure on the outside world. If a business venture fails, it is because the market was wrong for the product, or that the investors didn't put up enough money. If person is unable to launch their blog due to inability to get work done, they'll point the finger at just about anything other than themselves. The reality is, just as we have learned that we build momentum by cultivating a strong internal strength through discipline, motivation and habits, we also lose momentum due to internal weaknesses. Let's take a look at a few of the biggest internal roadblocks that we face as we seek to build momentum.

Lack of Responsibility:

Perhaps this is the biggest type of internal roadblock that we must face as we seek to build momentum. Oftentimes, we end up failing due to some kind of problem, but we often erroneously believe that the problem belongs to the world. We can often take the position of the victim and in doing so, we give up the power to troubleshoot the issues and figure out what went wrong. Instead of looking to fix what went wrong, we point the finger away from ourselves in the hopes that we can somehow avoid dealing with the shame and pain of having made a mistake.

Have you ever worked with a boss who refuses to take responsibility for his actions? It's often troublesome when you see that nothing is getting fixed, instead you see the company suffer because the boss is too busy trying to blame other people for the problem. If he took a moment to really consider who was in the wrong, he might come to realize it was his own shortcomings that caused the problem. And then, after that something miraculous happens. After you are willing to take responsibility for your failures, you will learn how you can improve upon them. This is the key to keeping momentum, primarily because momentum can be lost some times due to failure, but the only time that momentum comes to halt is when you give up responsibility.

Imagine that you were driving a car down the highway and you saw a brick wall several miles away, yet you slammed into it anyway. Would you blame the engine, the wall or yourself for failing to swerve out of the way? If you were to blame anyone except yourself, you very well might slam into that same brick wall a few days later after you get your car out of the shop. The only thing that outrights halt momentum is repeatedly running into the same obstacle over and over again, and that only happens when you refuse to look at your role in the failure.

It can be a painful feeling, to look at your own mistakes and own up to them, but that is how we grow as people. Yet so many of us are terrified of failure and the effects of it that we will do anything to avoid having to admit that we failed, which brings us to our next point.

Fear of Failure:

Failure is often punished twice in our culture. We are first punished with the effects of failure, such as a poor report card, bankruptcy or losing money, but then we are punished a second time with shame. That shame is often directed against us by other people, our parents, friends or superiors who want us to feel bad for having made a mistake in the first place. Our culture of punishing failure twice has led many a person to feel that failure is the worst possible thing that can happen in their lives. And so, they make a point to try and avoid failure at all costs. Yet, the reality is that failure oftentimes cannot be avoided because failure is a learning process. We often cannot achieve success without some kind of failure and so this creates a paradox. The only way we can reach success is to fail, yet so many people want to avoid failure entirely. This means that at the core, those who are afraid of failure will spend all of their effort and energy to avoid success. Confused? Think about it for a moment. If failure is truly the only way to become successful, then avoiding failure means you are avoiding success.

The fear of failure is a powerful fear, it often drives people into mediocrity. Most people would rather live an okay life and not risk anything, than to live a great life and risk failure. This is primarily because failure is punished twice. If you find that you are having trouble succeeding in your life, if you aren't able to keep your momentum up due to the fact that you are constantly giving up or aren't able to take sufficient risks, it might be because you are afraid of failure and that fear is stopping you from achieving the results that you want to achieve. The answer isn't to eliminate all possibility of failure, the answer is to learn that failure is not the worst thing that can happen. The worst thing that can happen is to never try.

Failure is a natural part of the success process and is a fantastic teacher, if you are willing to allow it to teach you the lessons that it has for you. By changing your perspective on failure and learning how to embrace it, you will find that you are far more capable to get things done. Oftentimes the things that kill our motivation and momentum can be fear, so by learning to change your perspective on the thing that is most scary to you, you are taking control of your own destiny. It's not particularly easy to change the way you look at fear, but remember, reacting poorly to failure is nothing more than a habit. The problem is that habit was usually deeply ingrained in us as we were growing up. We might have done something by accident, such as knocked over a lamp, or we could have gotten a poor report card, and then suddenly we are forced to deal with a ton of shame and blame that does nothing to inspire us to do better. Those kinds of wounds go deep and we begin to develop the habit of thinking of failure as a very bad thing. The reality is that failure can be one of the greatest gifts in the world, but you will never be able to get the momentum you are looking for unless you learn to look failure dead in the eye and embrace it as a teacher and a friend. The lessons might be painful, but they should never be shameful.

Emotional Factors:

Whether we like it or not, we must accept the fact that we are emotional creatures. More than that, our emotions often tend to have a major impact on our lives and our moods can determine how we feel, act and think. Yet, emotions and moods are temporary things. They can change at the drop of a hat, and worse yet, you can't particularly plan for a good or bad mood. They arrive unbidden and stay for an unknown duration. Yet, how many of us tend to get caught up in our emotions and allow them to make our decisions for us? We are feeling angry, so we get into a fight with our spouse. We're sad, so we don't bother to work on our big project.

Emotional regulation is a major issue for a lot of people. They tend to take each emotion and feeling as if it were the lens to which they view reality. So, if a person is in a good mood, they might be willing to work really hard, if they are in a sour mood, they might not want to work at all. The reality is that since moods are temporal and the work that we do is long lasting, we often find our momentum threatened by how we feel at any given time. This can be problematic if you're going through a relatively emotional time, such as dealing with conflict at home or with a friend. By letting your moods run the show, you are setting yourself up for long-term momentum loss due to the fact that you really have little control over what your emotions are going to be like in the long term. You can't particularly plan how you want to feel a week from now. You can't say "on Wednesday I'll be angry, on Friday I'll be happy and then Sunday is going to be a mopey kind of day." That would be ridiculous. What's even more ridiculous, however, is the fact that while we know we cannot plan for moods to shift, we often do not account for those mood swings.

What I mean by that is the fact that when an emotion changes inside of us, we often tend to just go with it. We act as if we have to follow how our emotions make us feel. The reality is that the opposite is actually true. Our emotions tend to follow our actions. For example, if you are in a really angry mood, you have several options. You can give into your emotional impetus to be full of rage and swear, curse and yell. You can try to ignore your feelings and shove them deep down, causing more emotional trouble over time, or you can make the conscious decision to acknowledge your feelings but refuse to allow them to dictate your actions. Make no mistake: this is a very hard thing to do. We are often taught that we have no choice when it comes to indulging our emotions, but the reality is that our emotions are somewhat like a toddler. It will make loud demands, but it has no real power over you. Whenever you give into that emotion's demands, you are just making it stronger and more spoiled, just like a child. But whenever you acknowledge the feelings but resist the pull to follow after them, you have a choice to change how you act.

Instead of acting upon the emotion that you have, you might find that it would be far more useful to act upon the emotion that you want to have. For example, if you feel sad and listless, it might be a better idea to act as if you were upbeat and cheerful. Turn on some good music or find something that will inspire you. You don't have to obey your emotions just because they show up. Now, please note that this isn't about long term emotional struggles such as psychological or mood disorders. The solution to dealing with depression isn't to just "cheer up." The reality is that if you find that you are dealing with a complex psychological or emotional disorder, it might be in your best interest to invest some time and energy into getting some kind of professional counseling or therapy. No amount of wishing will put those disorders to rest.

But if you're just dealing with the occasional bad mood, as most of us have to deal with, it is far better for you to acknowledge how you feel but refuse to give into the mood's demands. Instead, do the thing that you would normally do. Try to give thanks when you are feeling desperate and hopeless, spend some time meditating or reading when you feel angry. Do anything that you can to avoid allowing your emotions to control you. You are allowed to have your emotions, they are necessary and important for human survival, even if they don't feel particularly pleasant. You aren't allowed, however, to allow your emotions to control you, because that would be akin to a toddler telling its parents how to live their lives. It would be nothing short of a recipe for absolute disaster.

Misery:

The cold and harsh reality is that sometimes a person is doing something out of a sense of obligation and not because they deeply desire to get it done. These people often try to convince themselves that they can somehow become more productive if they just try harder, but the reality is that these types of people need to find fields of work where they are much happier. It's one thing to be struggling with an aspect of a job or project, but it is an entirely different roadblock when the individual hates what they are doing. There is no magic bullet to make a person suddenly love their job and there is no magic bullet that will allow for a person to suddenly start caring about whatever task is before them.

Some people who are working on major projects often feel a deep sense of disconnection with their work and the reason why they feel that disconnect is because their motives aren't particularly pure. This means that they should either do one of two things. The first option would be to look at their motives and see if they can change them so that they are good and proper. Someone purely motivated by money might not have the juice to finish out a massive project and would quickly lose momentum.

The second option would be to entirely abandon the project or job and move onto something that will make you happy. Obligation can really kill momentum and that momentum usually doesn't come back.

Conclusion

Momentum is one of the most important parts of being a high-performing member of society. When you learn to increase your momentum through developing good habits, focus on building up your discipline and learning how to increase your motivation on a daily basis, you will find that you can get far more done than you ever thought possible. The real solution is to focus on achieving as much good as you can every single day and avoiding the many different pitfalls that can kill that momentum. Focus, stay consistent and whatever you do, don't blame the external circumstances for your internal problems.

Other books available by Landon T. Smith on Kindle, paperback and audio:

How to Outmaneuver and Outsmart Anyone: Time Tested Strategies That Will Give You the Upper Hand When Dealing With People

www.ingramcontent.com/pod-product-compliance
Lightning Source LLC
Chambersburg PA
CBHW021017180526
45163CB00005B/1986